SPIDERS, TICKS, MITES, SCORPIONS AND MORE

INSECTS FOR KIDS
ARACHNID EDITION
CHILDREN'S BUG & SPIDER BOOKS

Speedy Publishing LLC
40 E. Main St. #1156
Newark, DE 19711
www.speedypublishing.com
Copyright 2017

All Rights reserved. No part of this book may be reproduced or used in any way or form or by any means whether electronic or mechanical, this means that you cannot record or photocopy any material ideas or tips that are provided in this book.

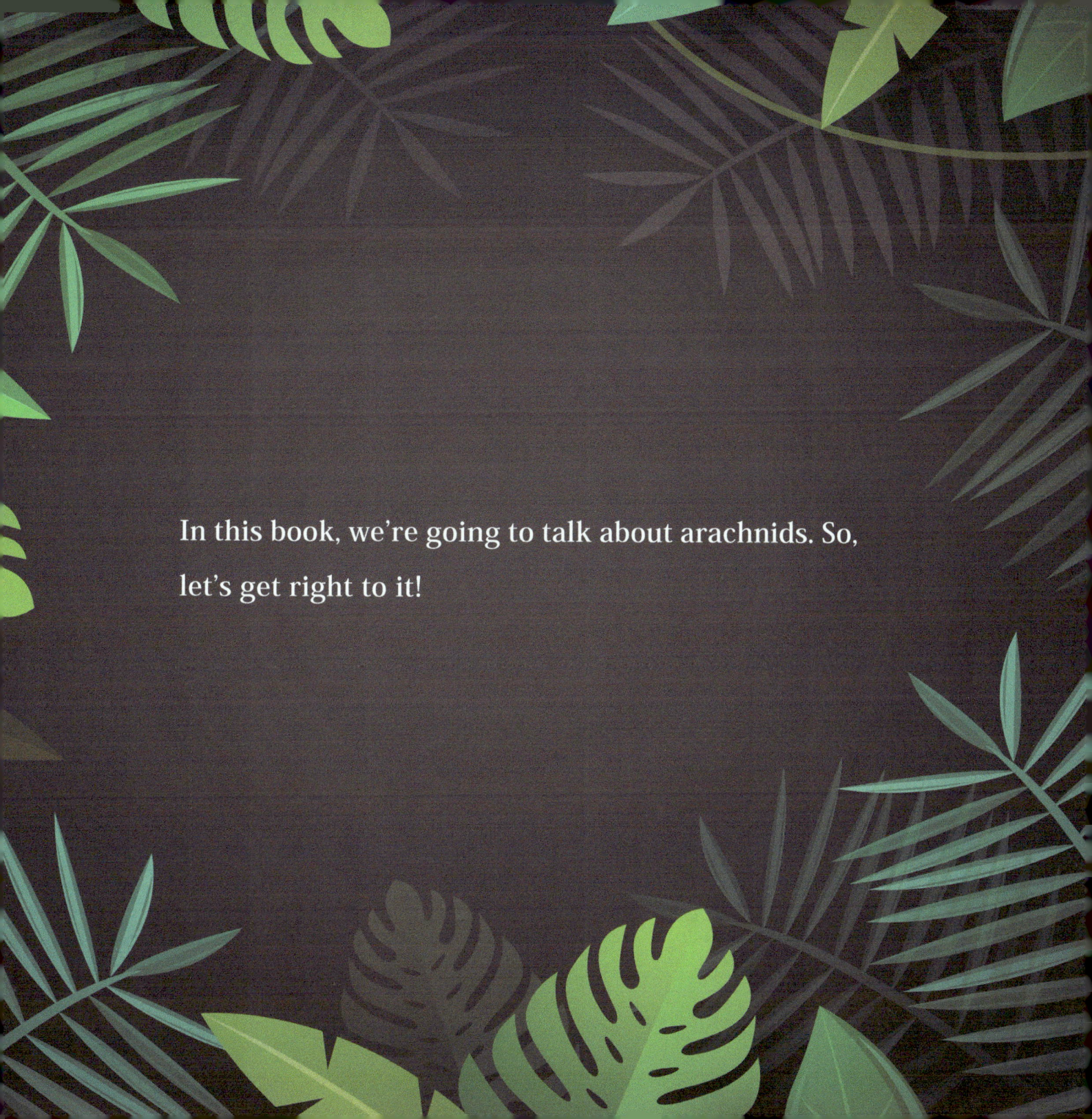

In this book, we're going to talk about arachnids. So, let's get right to it!

Many people mistakenly categorize spiders as types of insects, however they're not insects at all. Spiders belong to a class of animals called arachnids. Arachnids are easy to distinguish from insects because they have a completely different body structure.

Insects have six legs and arachnids have eight. Insects have three body parts: the head, the thorax, and the abdomen. Arachnids have only two, which consists of a joined head and thorax as one part and their abdomens as the second part.

Insects and arachnids move very differently from each other as well. If you've ever watched how an ant, which is an insect, moves compared to the way a spider, which is an arachnid, moves, you would clearly see the difference. Lots of insects have wings, but there aren't any arachnids with wings.

Arachnids don't undergo a complete process of metamorphosis like insects do. Instead, they go through what is called an incomplete metamorphosis.

When they hatch out of their eggs, they are just much smaller versions of their adult bodies. They do change as they go through each stage of growth, but at each stage they still look like their adult bodies only smaller.

Ancestors of the arachnids have been on Earth for more than 500 million years!

Spiders as well as ticks, mites, and scorpions all belong to the class of arachnids.

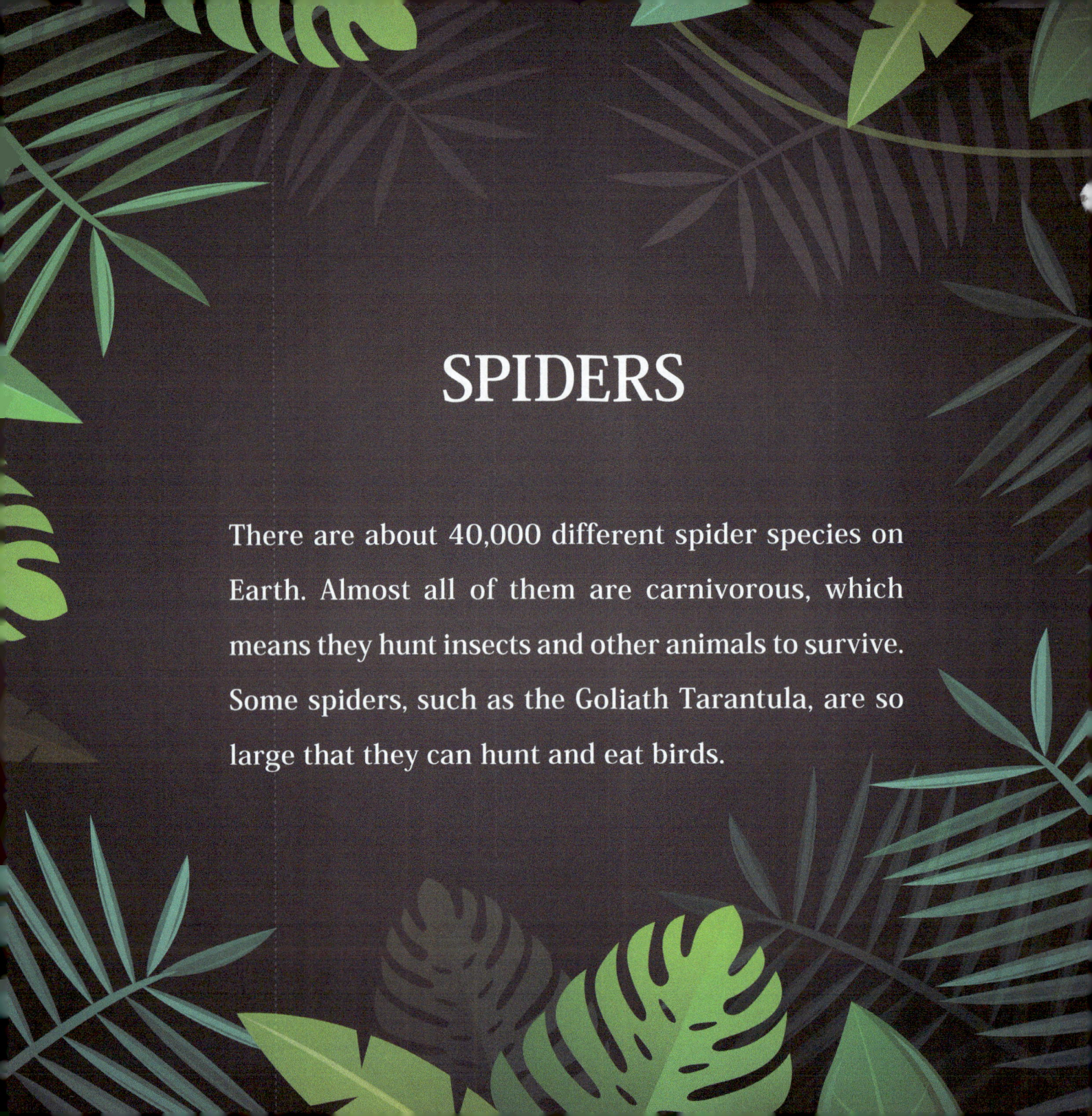

SPIDERS

There are about 40,000 different spider species on Earth. Almost all of them are carnivorous, which means they hunt insects and other animals to survive. Some spiders, such as the Goliath Tarantula, are so large that they can hunt and eat birds.

GOLIATH TARANTULA

In most cases, male spiders are smaller than female spiders. The bodies of spiders differ from other types of arachnids because their joined heads and thoraxes, a structure called the cephalothorax, are separated from their abdomens by a defined waist that's narrow.

Spiders have a lot of different body parts with different functions that make up the cephalothorax.

They are: The spider's eyes, most spiders have eight; Its mouth with its fangs, which deliver poison to its victims; Its poison glands; Its stomach; Its brain.

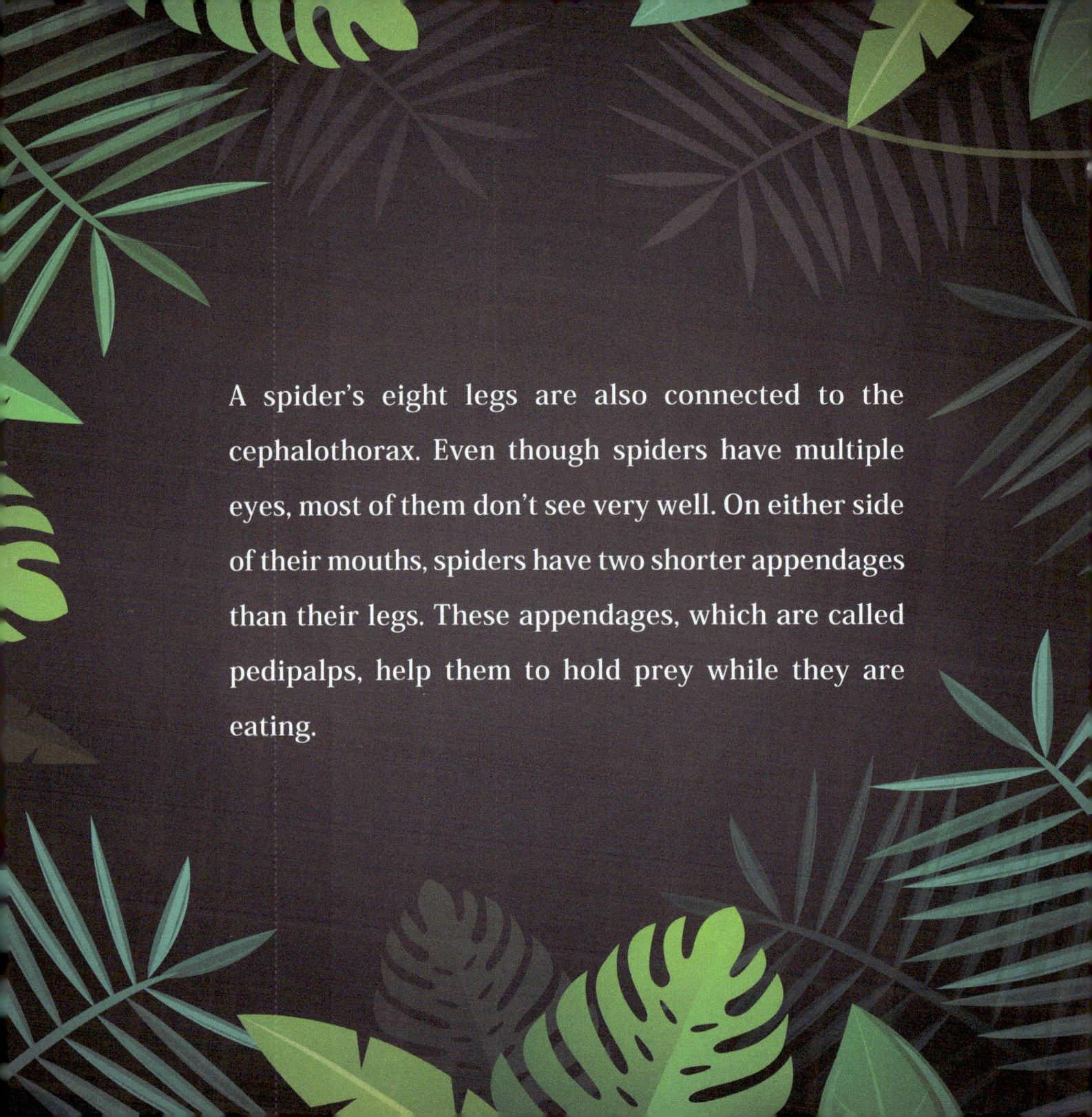

A spider's eight legs are also connected to the cephalothorax. Even though spiders have multiple eyes, most of them don't see very well. On either side of their mouths, spiders have two shorter appendages than their legs. These appendages, which are called pedipalps, help them to hold prey while they are eating.

Most spiders have very hairy legs. Their hairs sense vibrations and they can also sense different smells. At the end of each leg there are two or more claws. Each of their legs has six joints, which means that spiders have 48 "knees."

The second portion of a spider's body is its abdomen. At the abdomen's back end is where the glands that produce silk are located. These are called the spinnerets.

Each of the glands creates a different type of silk. Some of the silk is very sticky and other silk is very fine. Each type of silk is specific for building different sections of the spider's web.

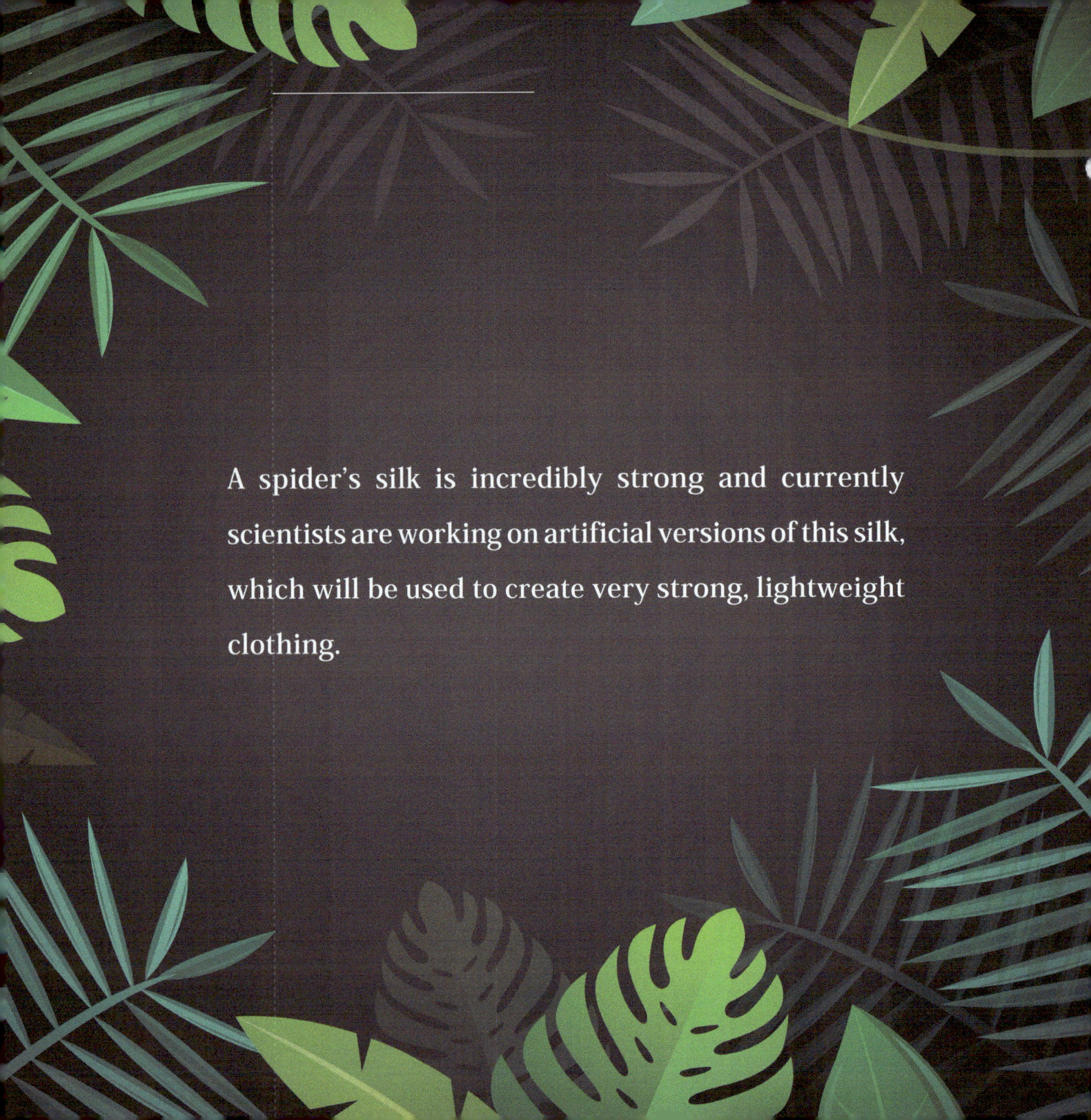

A spider's silk is incredibly strong and currently scientists are working on artificial versions of this silk, which will be used to create very strong, lightweight clothing.

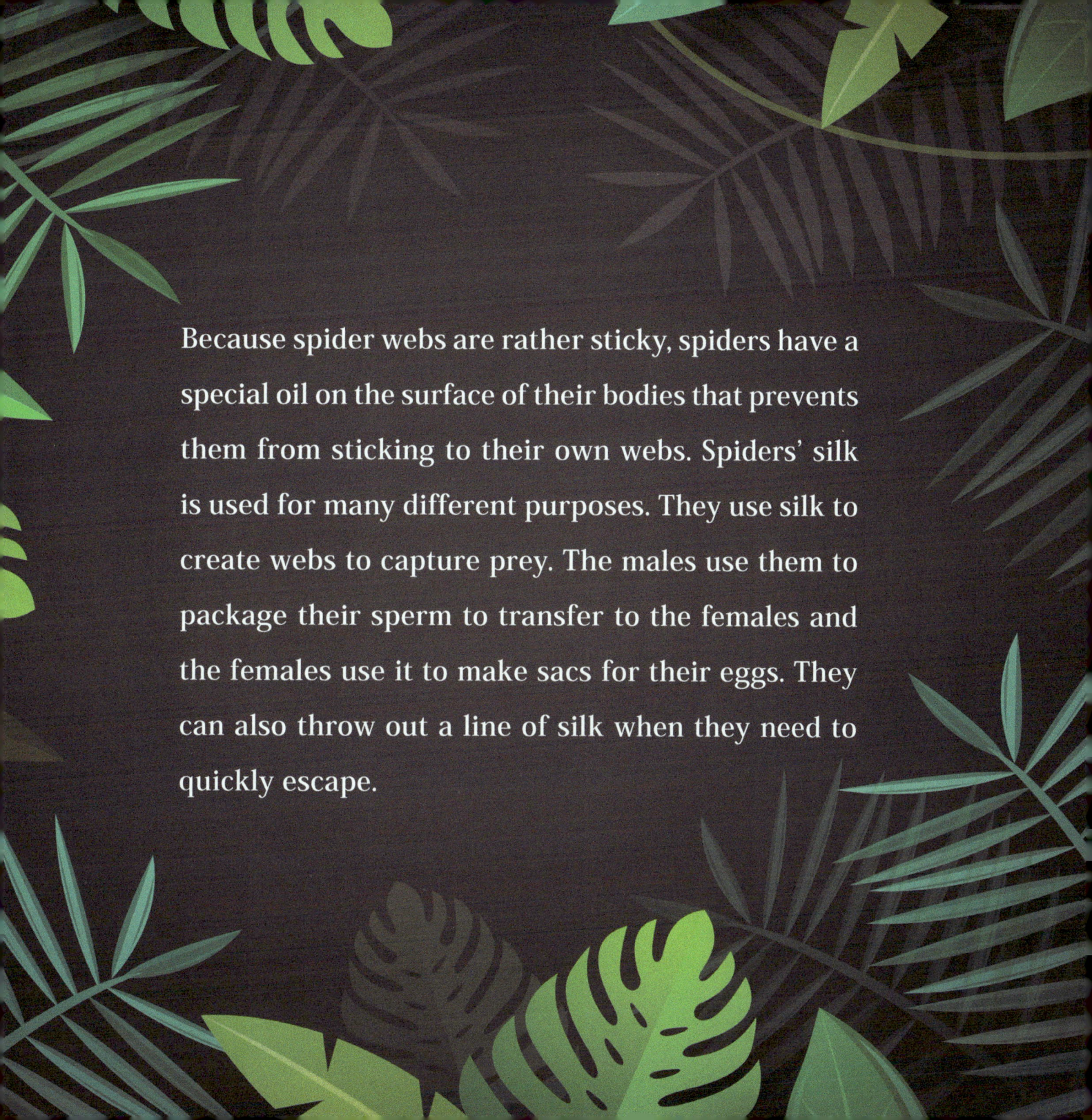

Because spider webs are rather sticky, spiders have a special oil on the surface of their bodies that prevents them from sticking to their own webs. Spiders' silk is used for many different purposes. They use silk to create webs to capture prey. The males use them to package their sperm to transfer to the females and the females use it to make sacs for their eggs. They can also throw out a line of silk when they need to quickly escape.

All spiders manufacture silk, but not all of them weave webs from their silk. Each species of spider weaves a different type of web, but their webs fall into three categories: orbs, sheets, and funnels.

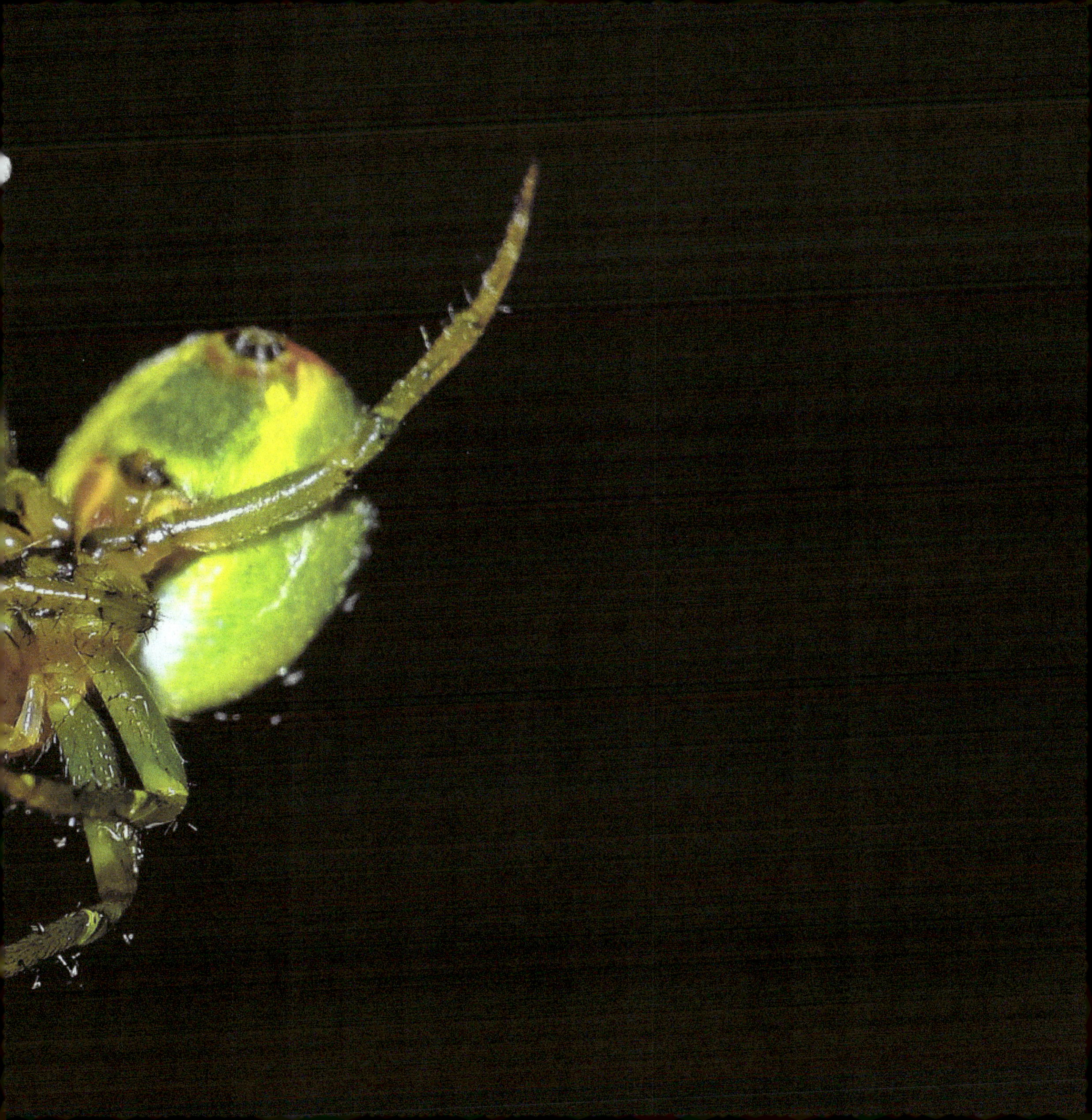

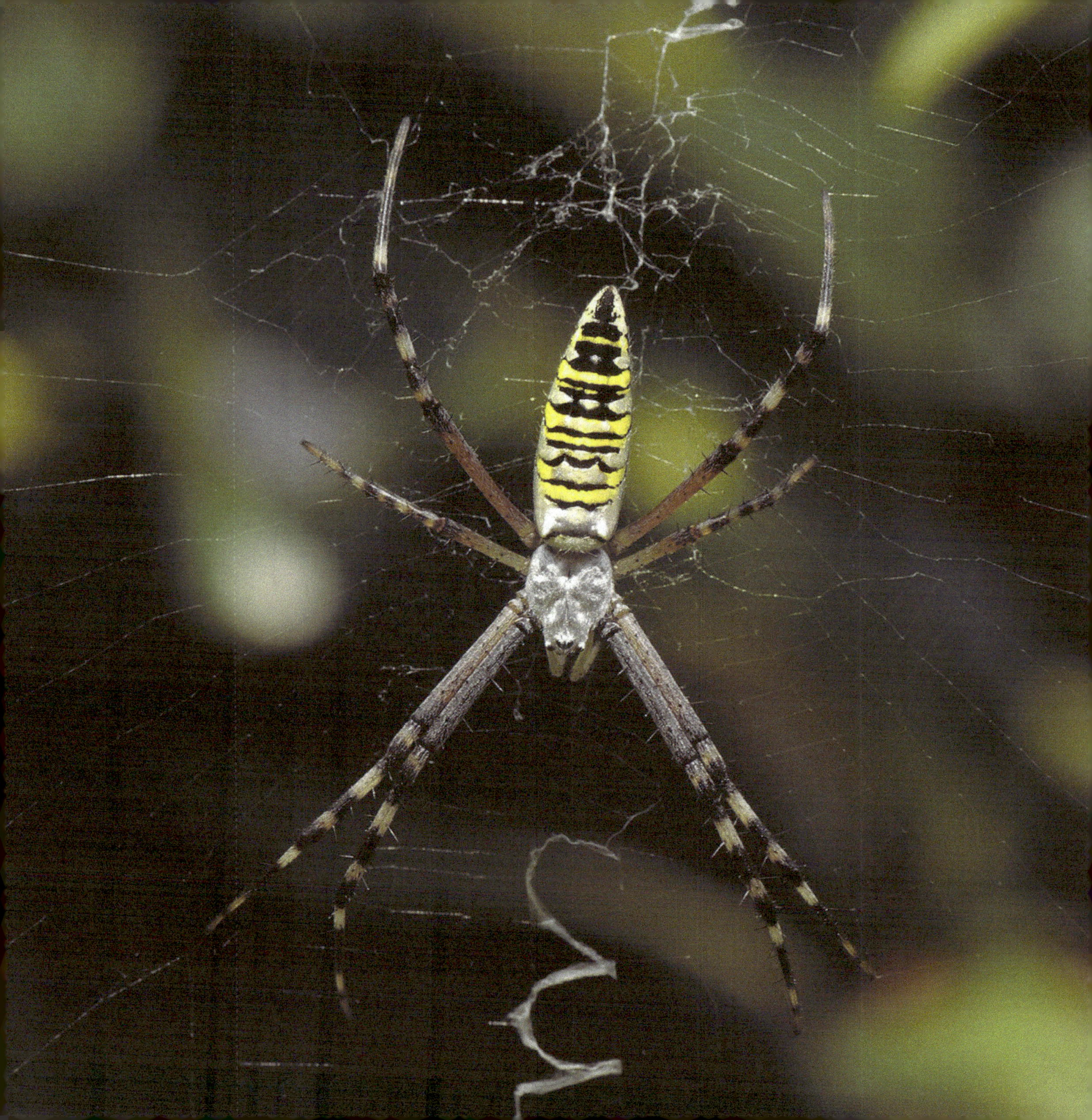

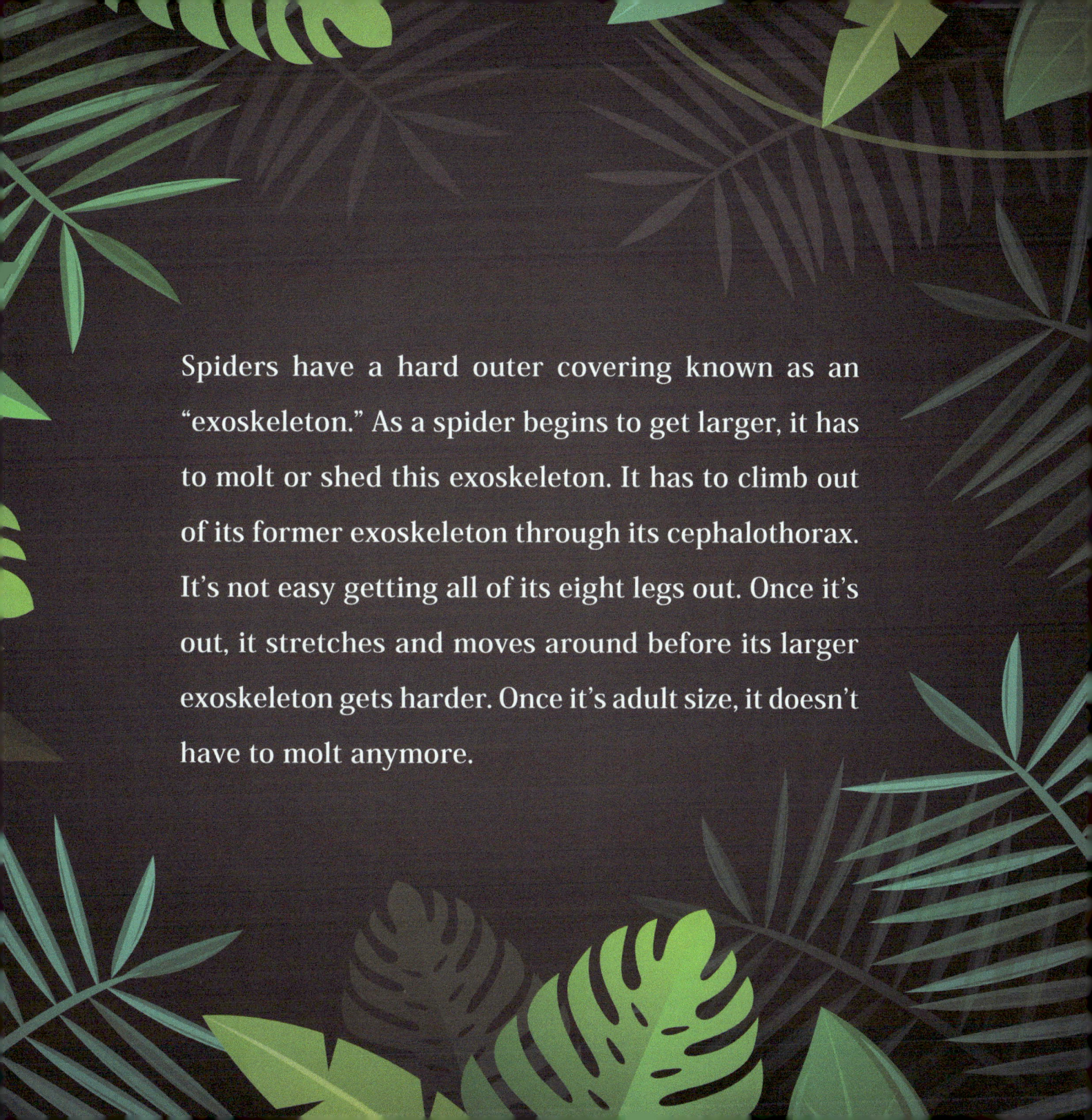

Spiders have a hard outer covering known as an "exoskeleton." As a spider begins to get larger, it has to molt or shed this exoskeleton. It has to climb out of its former exoskeleton through its cephalothorax. It's not easy getting all of its eight legs out. Once it's out, it stretches and moves around before its larger exoskeleton gets harder. Once it's adult size, it doesn't have to molt anymore.

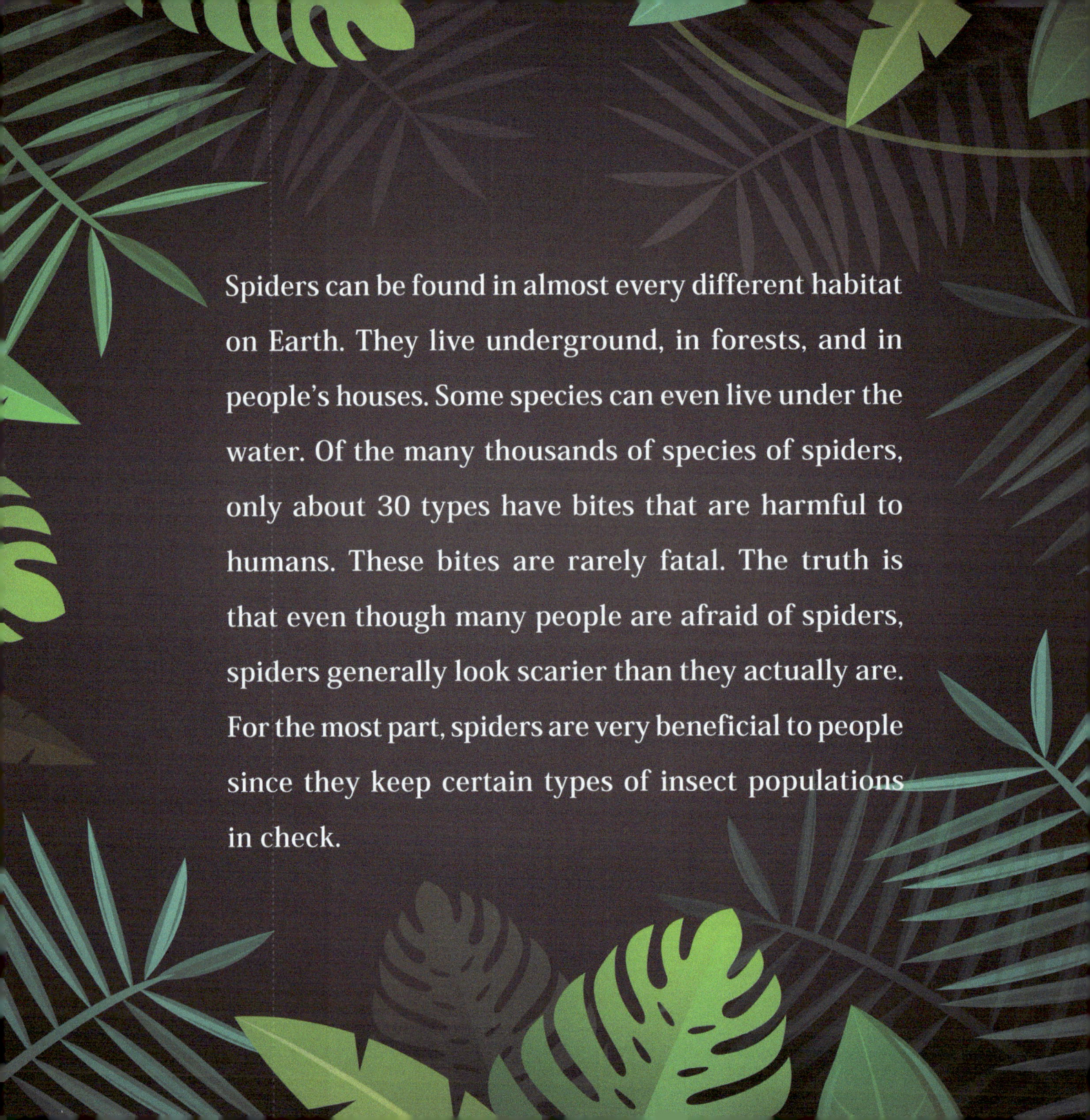

Spiders can be found in almost every different habitat on Earth. They live underground, in forests, and in people's houses. Some species can even live under the water. Of the many thousands of species of spiders, only about 30 types have bites that are harmful to humans. These bites are rarely fatal. The truth is that even though many people are afraid of spiders, spiders generally look scarier than they actually are. For the most part, spiders are very beneficial to people since they keep certain types of insect populations in check.

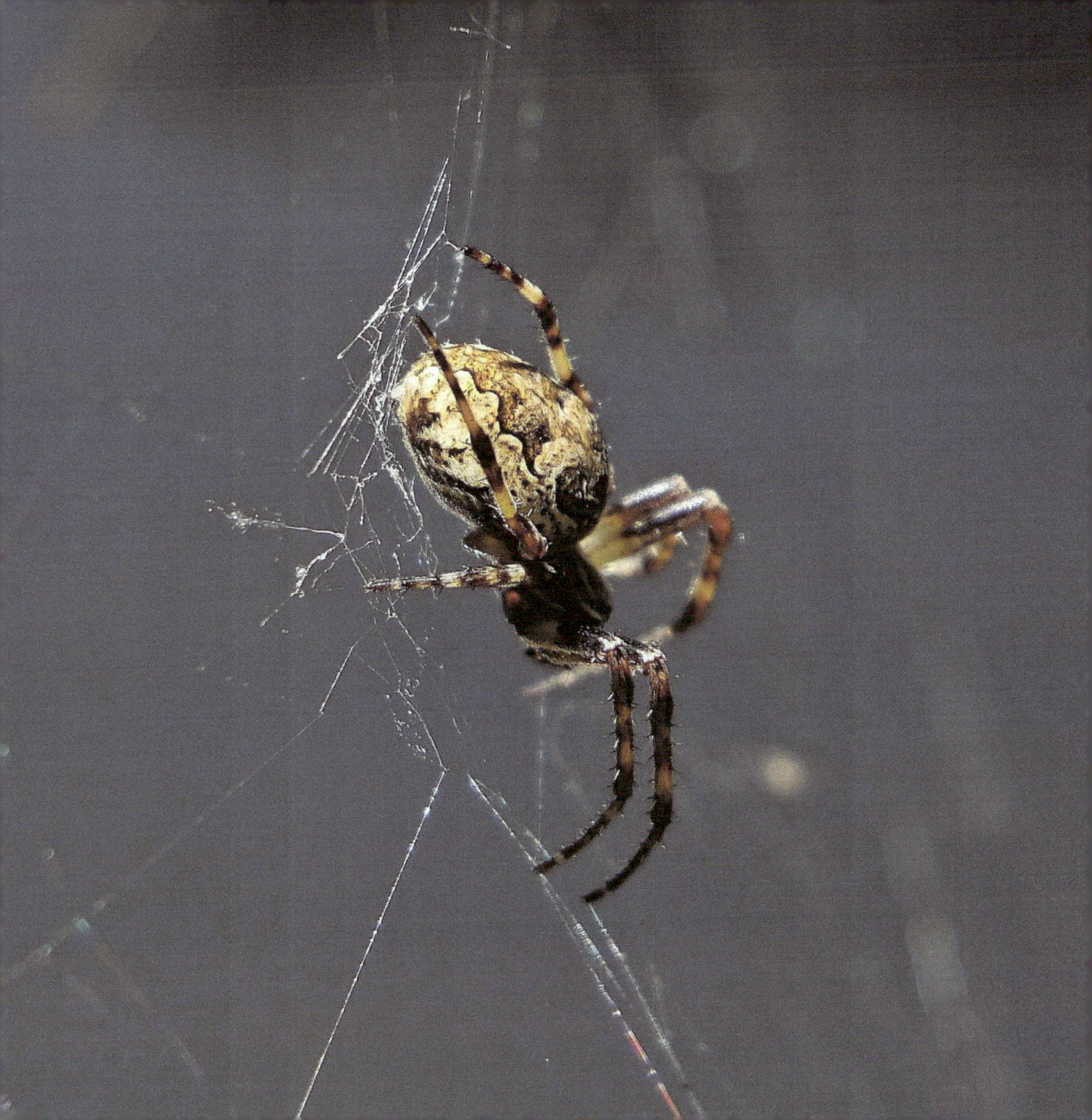

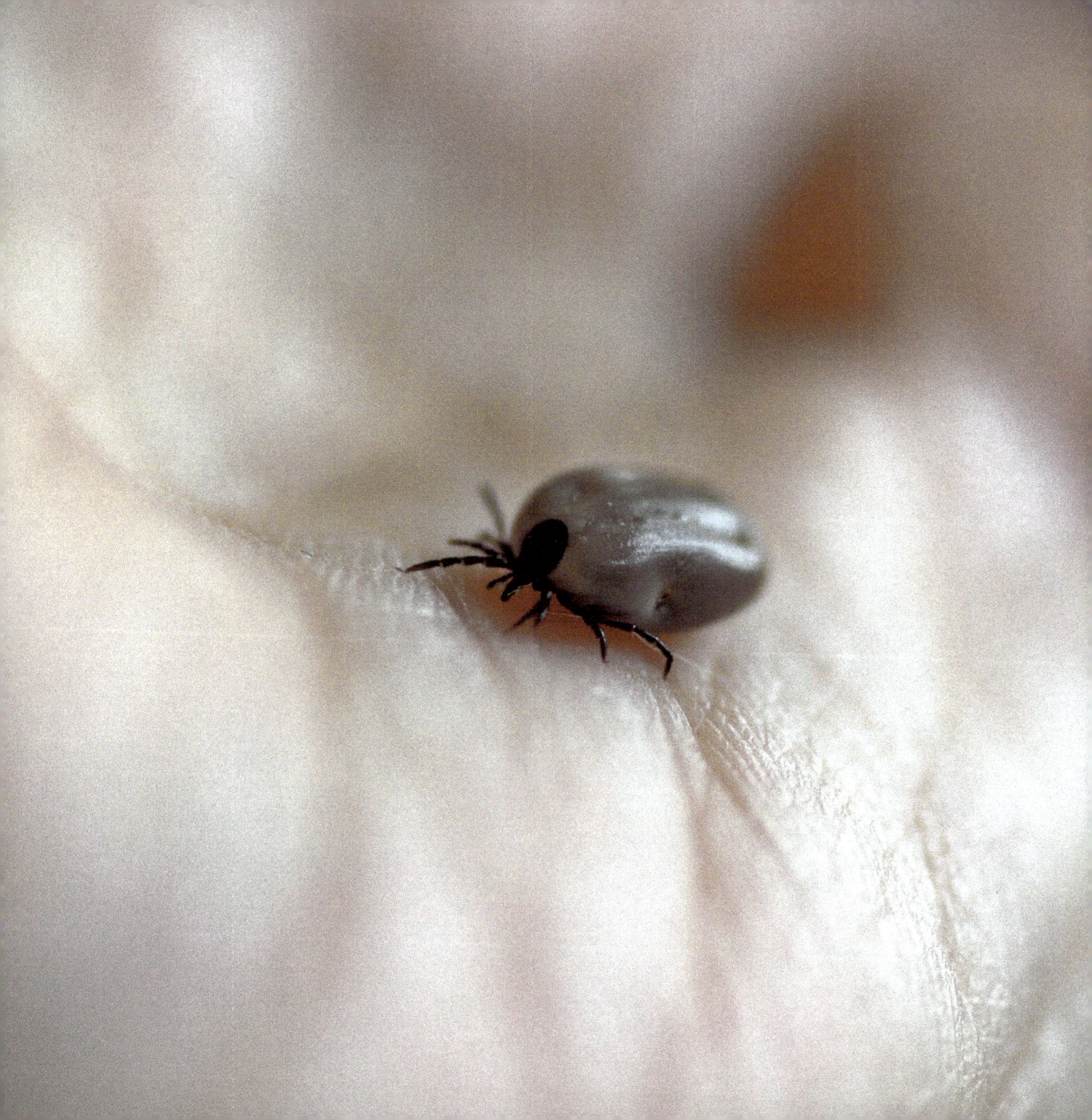

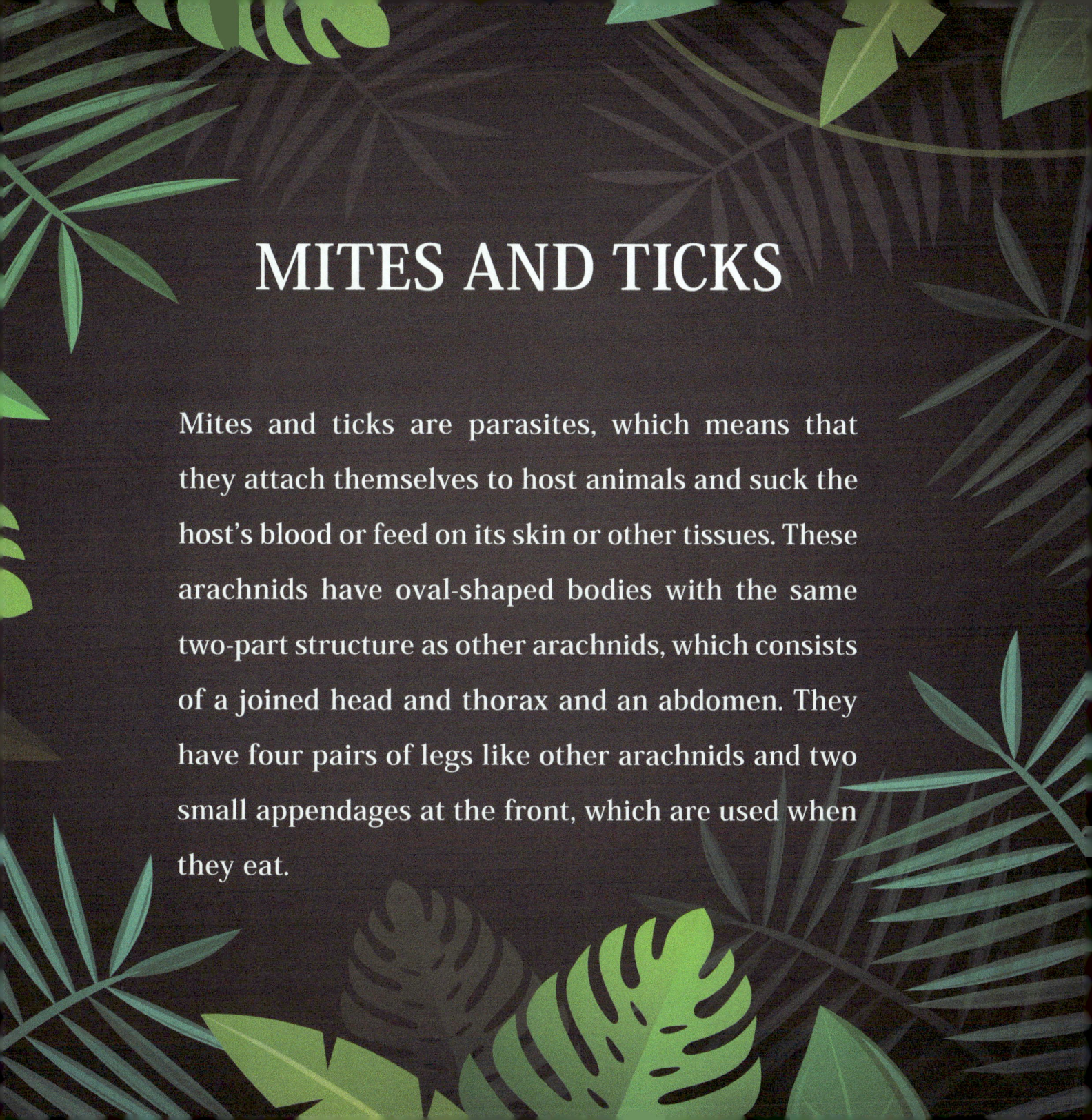

MITES AND TICKS

Mites and ticks are parasites, which means that they attach themselves to host animals and suck the host's blood or feed on its skin or other tissues. These arachnids have oval-shaped bodies with the same two-part structure as other arachnids, which consists of a joined head and thorax and an abdomen. They have four pairs of legs like other arachnids and two small appendages at the front, which are used when they eat.

Most species of mites and ticks are very tiny. Mites are microscopic and most ticks are as small as 0.2 of an inch to as large as 1 inch in length. Mites and ticks that have reached their adult stage have four pairs of legs, but at their earlier larval stage they only have three pairs of legs.

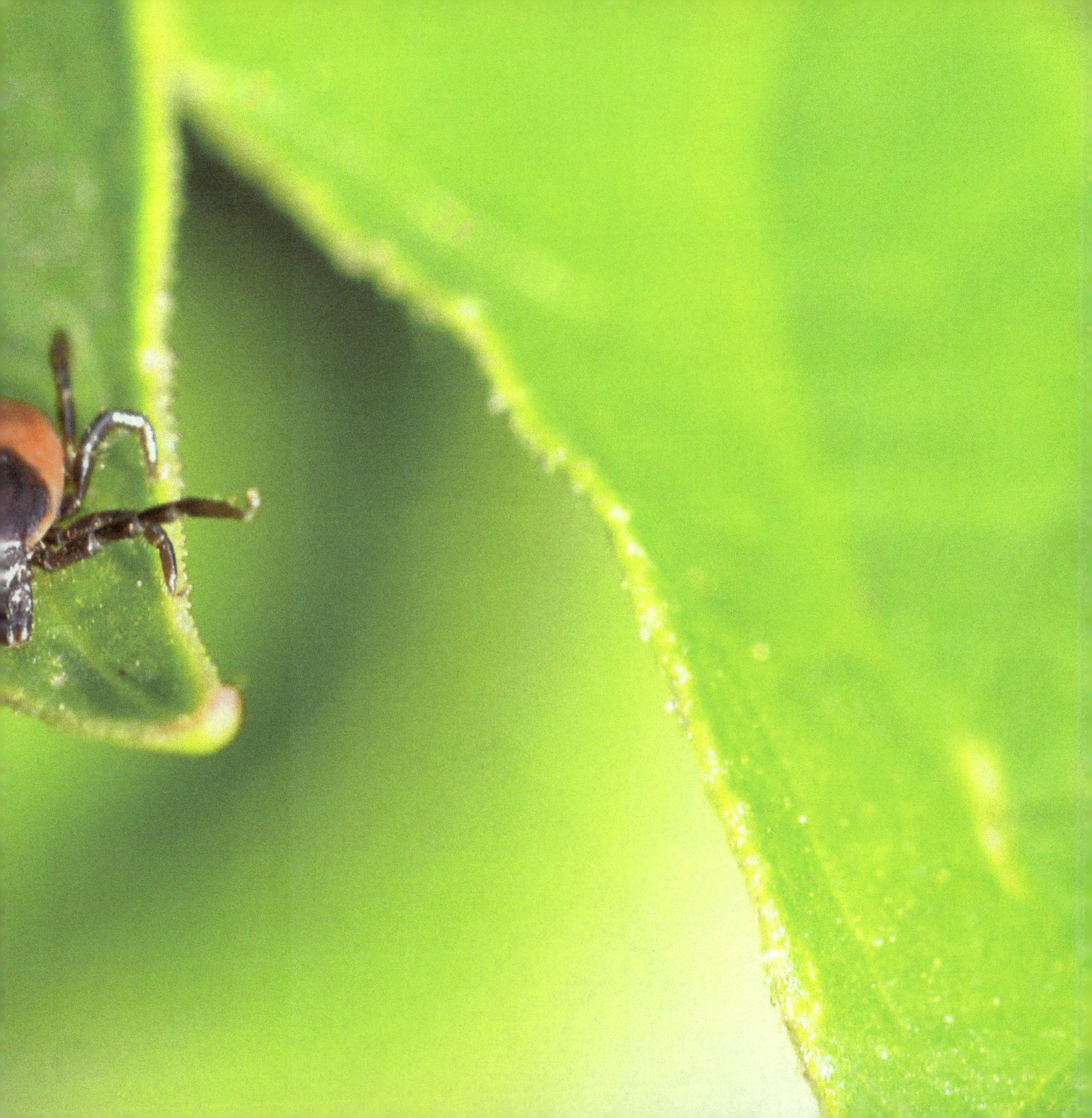

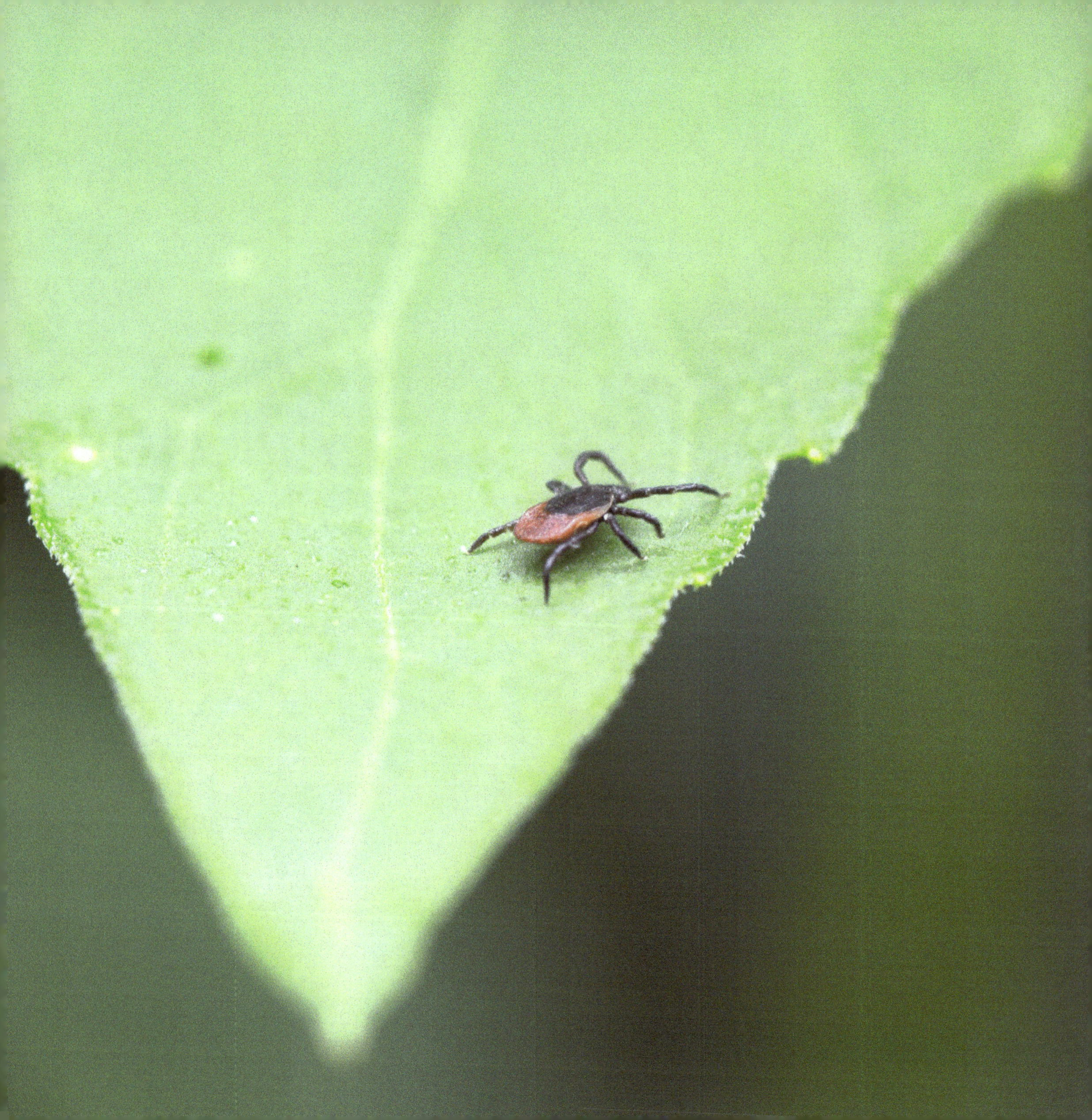

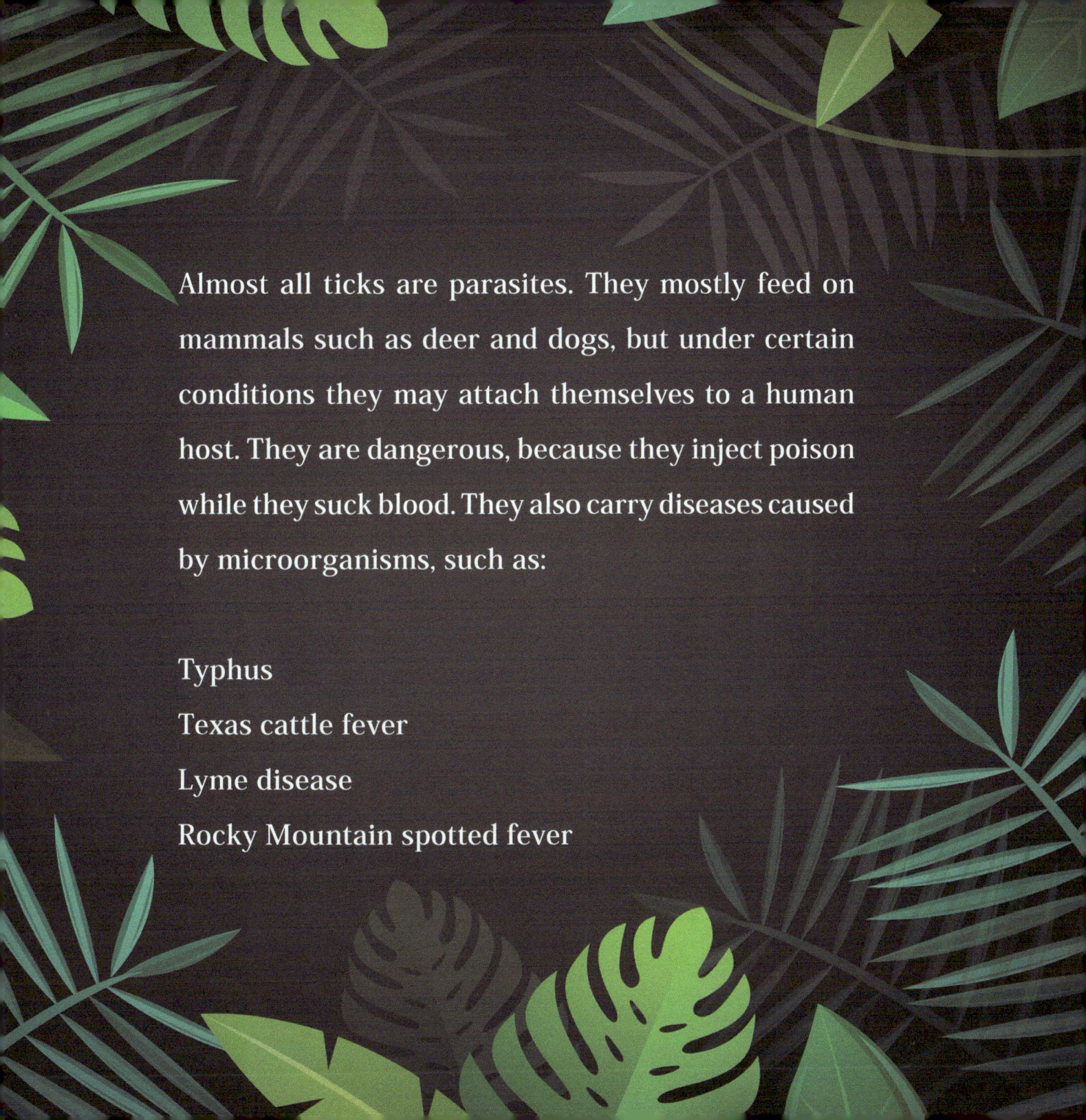

Almost all ticks are parasites. They mostly feed on mammals such as deer and dogs, but under certain conditions they may attach themselves to a human host. They are dangerous, because they inject poison while they suck blood. They also carry diseases caused by microorganisms, such as:

Typhus

Texas cattle fever

Lyme disease

Rocky Mountain spotted fever

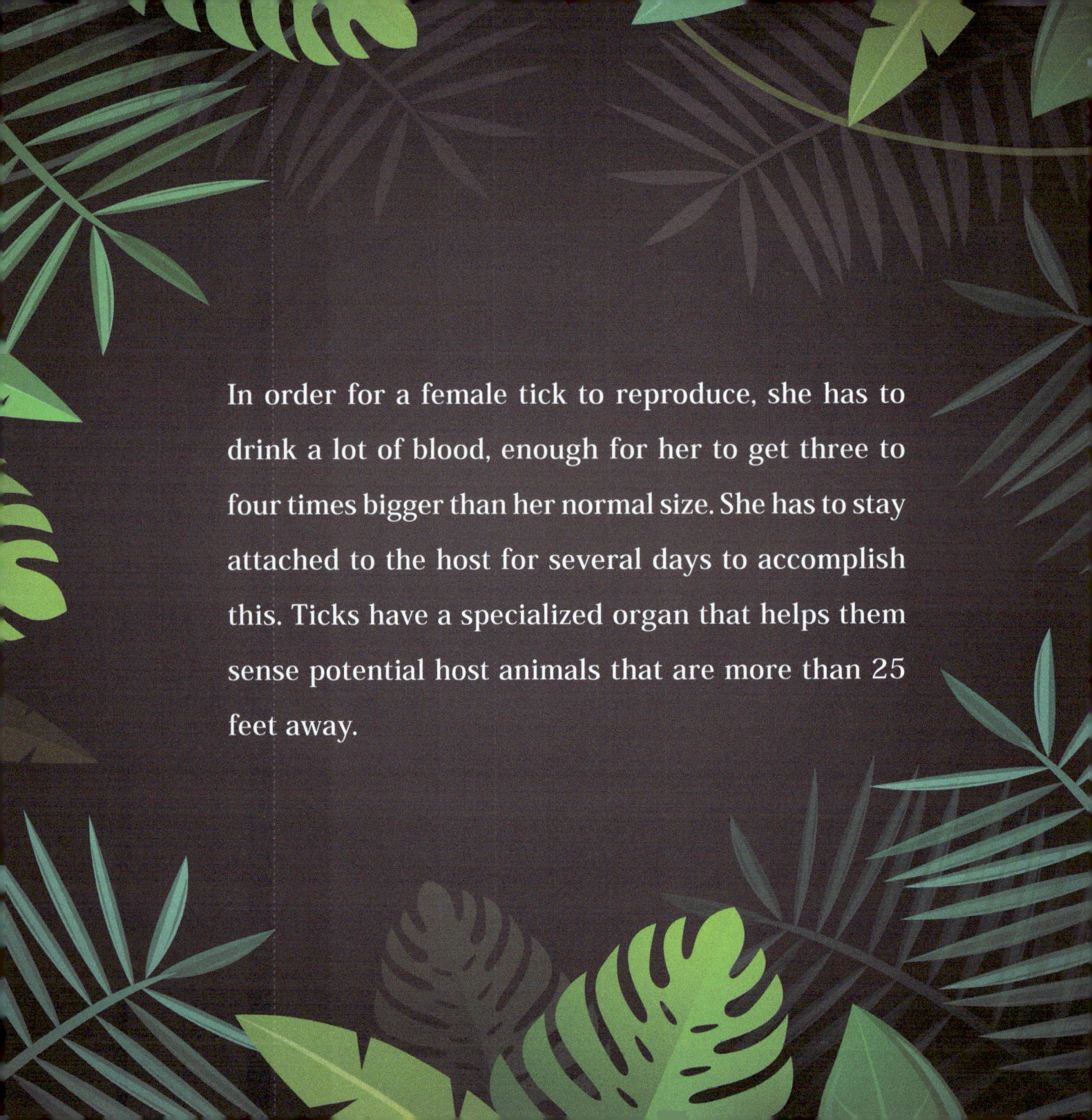

In order for a female tick to reproduce, she has to drink a lot of blood, enough for her to get three to four times bigger than her normal size. She has to stay attached to the host for several days to accomplish this. Ticks have a specialized organ that helps them sense potential host animals that are more than 25 feet away.

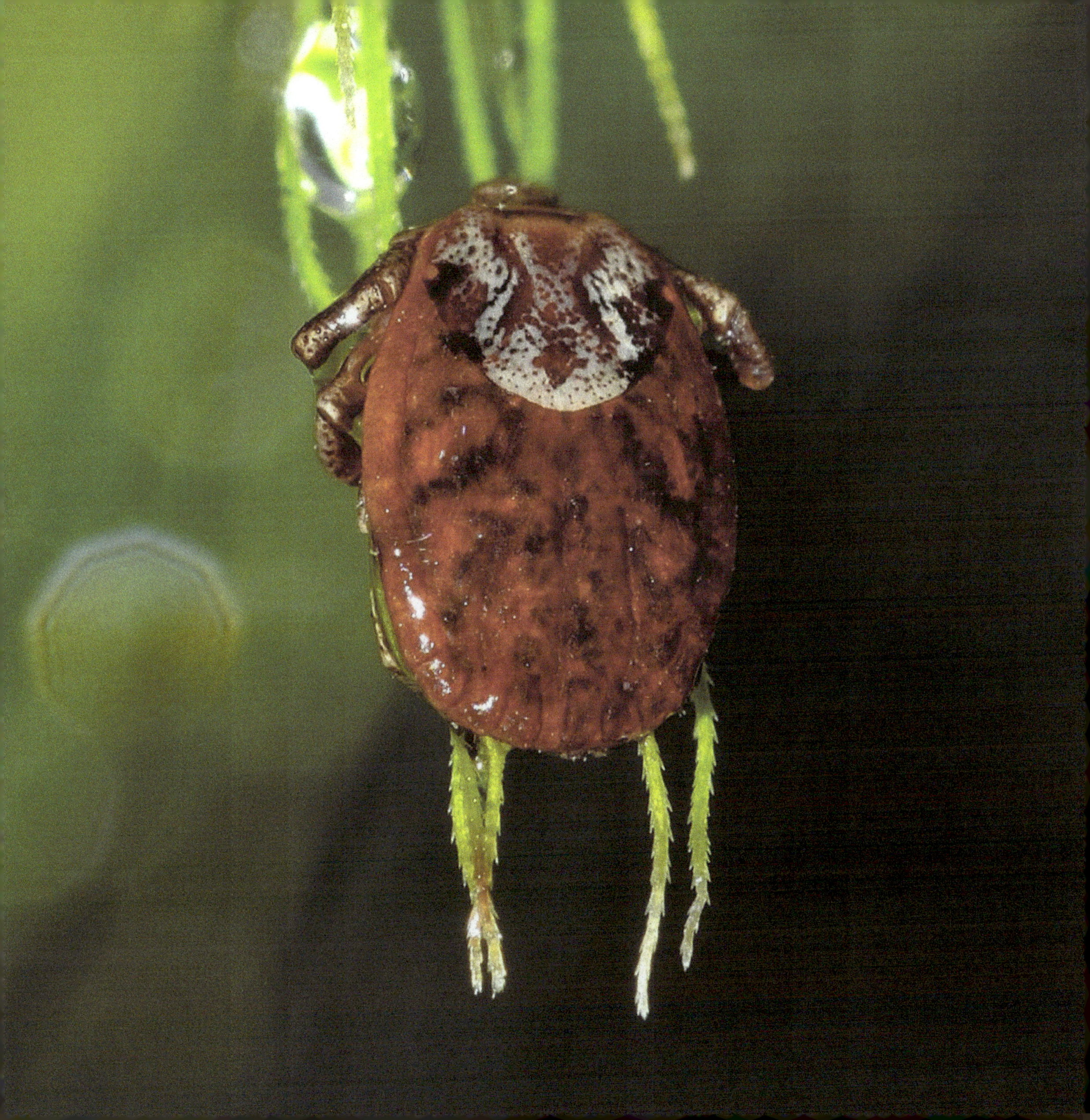

Birds and mammals that live outdoors are frequently attacked by mites. Mites can feed on the surface of their skin or their inside tissues. They sometimes dig under the host's skin and live and reproduce there. They carry diseases from microorganisms and also cause skin diseases that are contagious with symptoms like irritation and severe itching. Some mites, such as dust mites, aren't parasites but still cause allergic reactions.

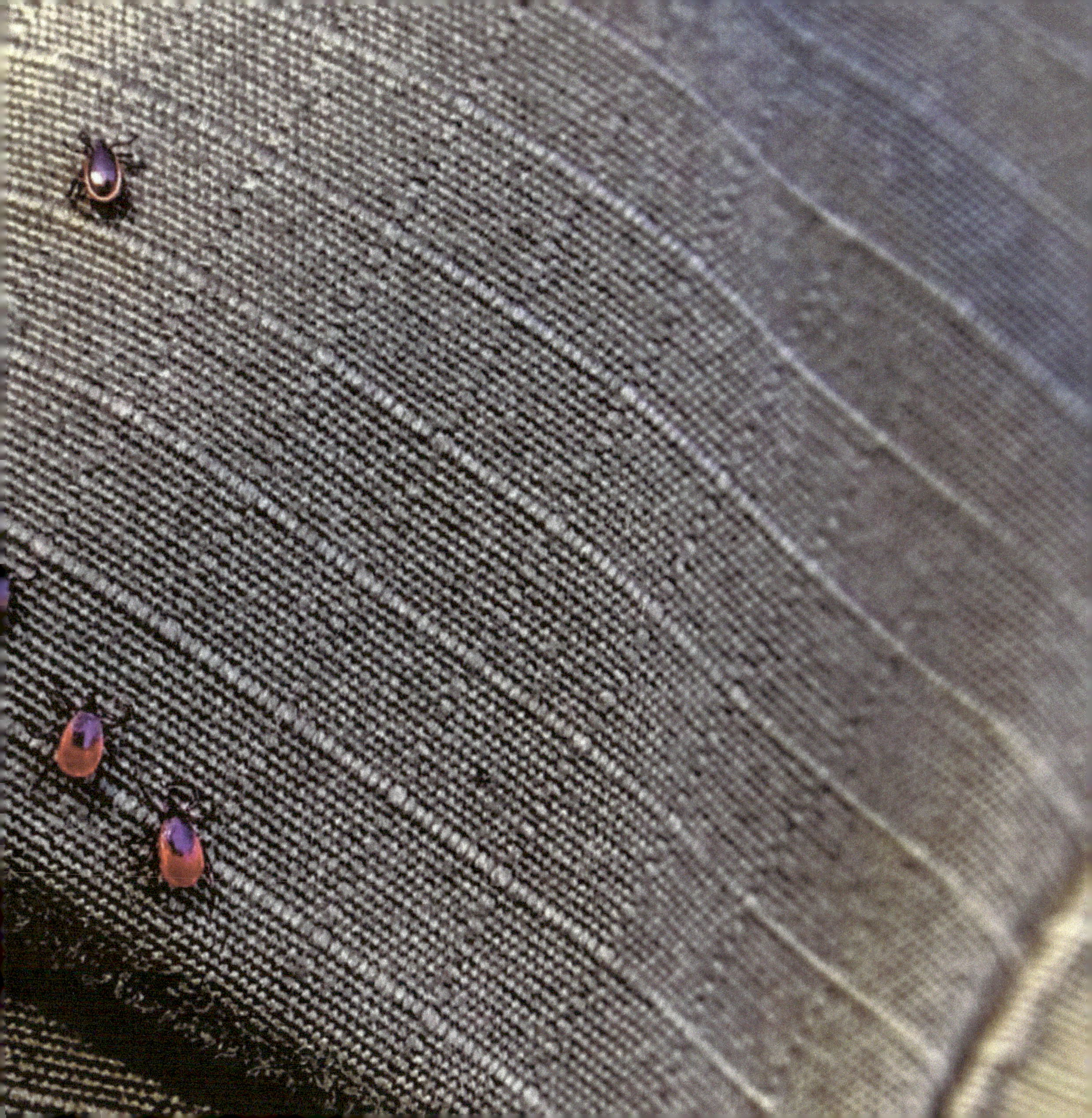

SCORPIONS

Scorpions look quite different than other types of arachnids. They have eight legs and their pedipalps are two enormous pincers. They also have narrow tails with segments that frequently curve over their backs. The ends of their tails have stingers that contain venom. They can attack insects with their pincers in the front.

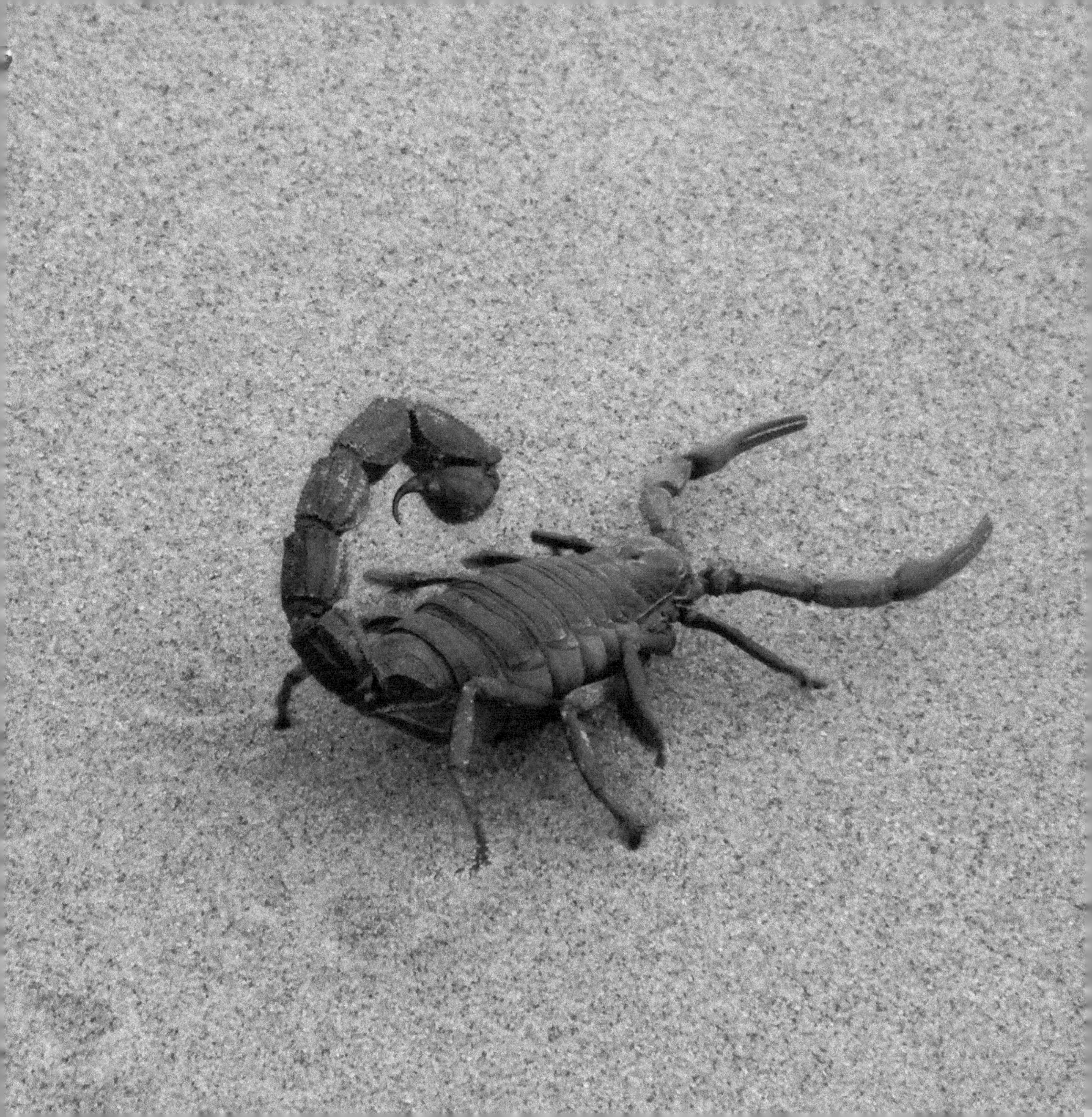

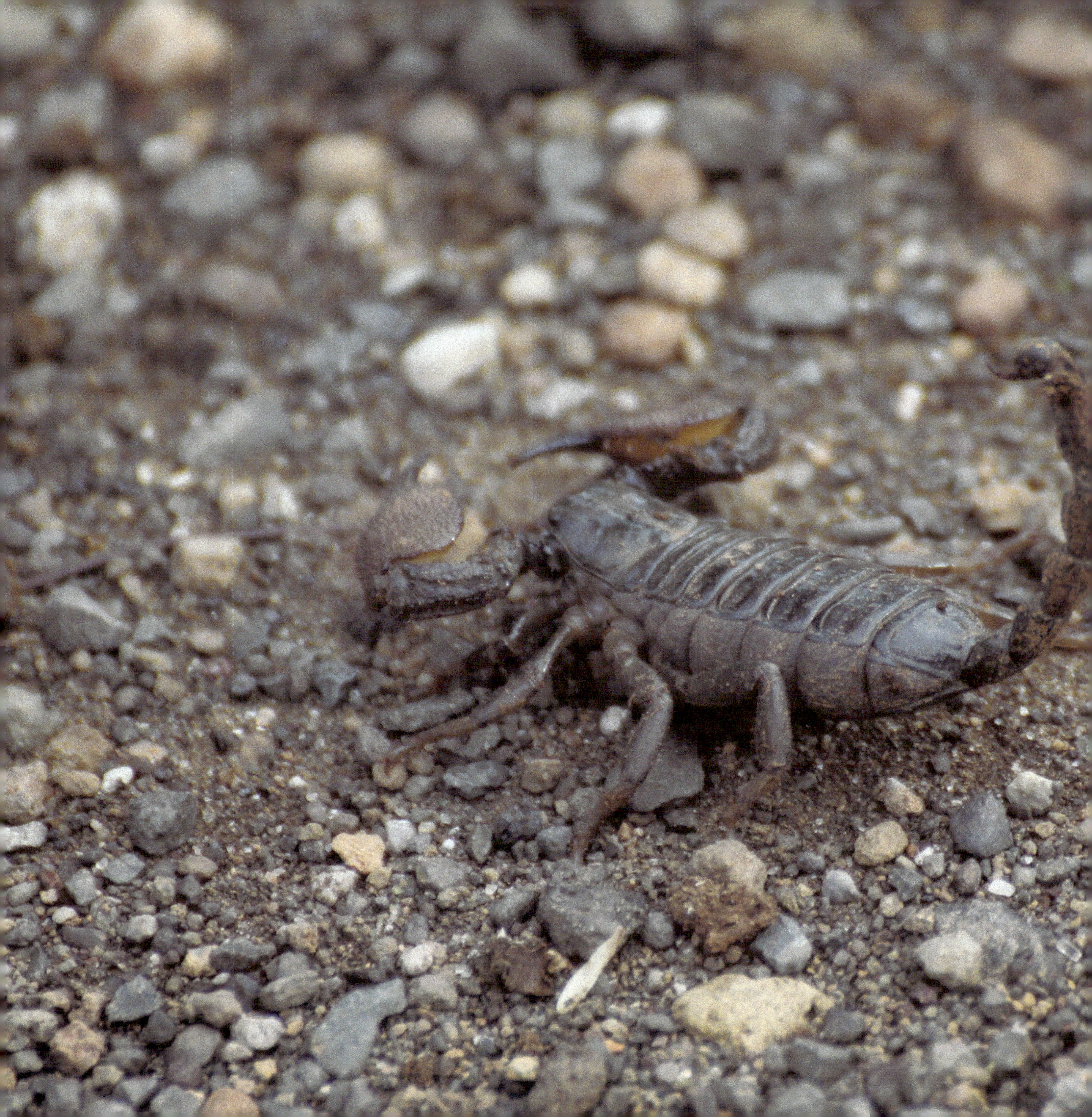

Then, they whip their tails from back to front to quickly sting their prey with venom to immobilize it before they eat it. They also use their powerful stingers to defend themselves against attackers. Most types of scorpions don't pose a severe threat to humans, but there are about 30-40 types worldwide that contain enough venom to kill a human being.

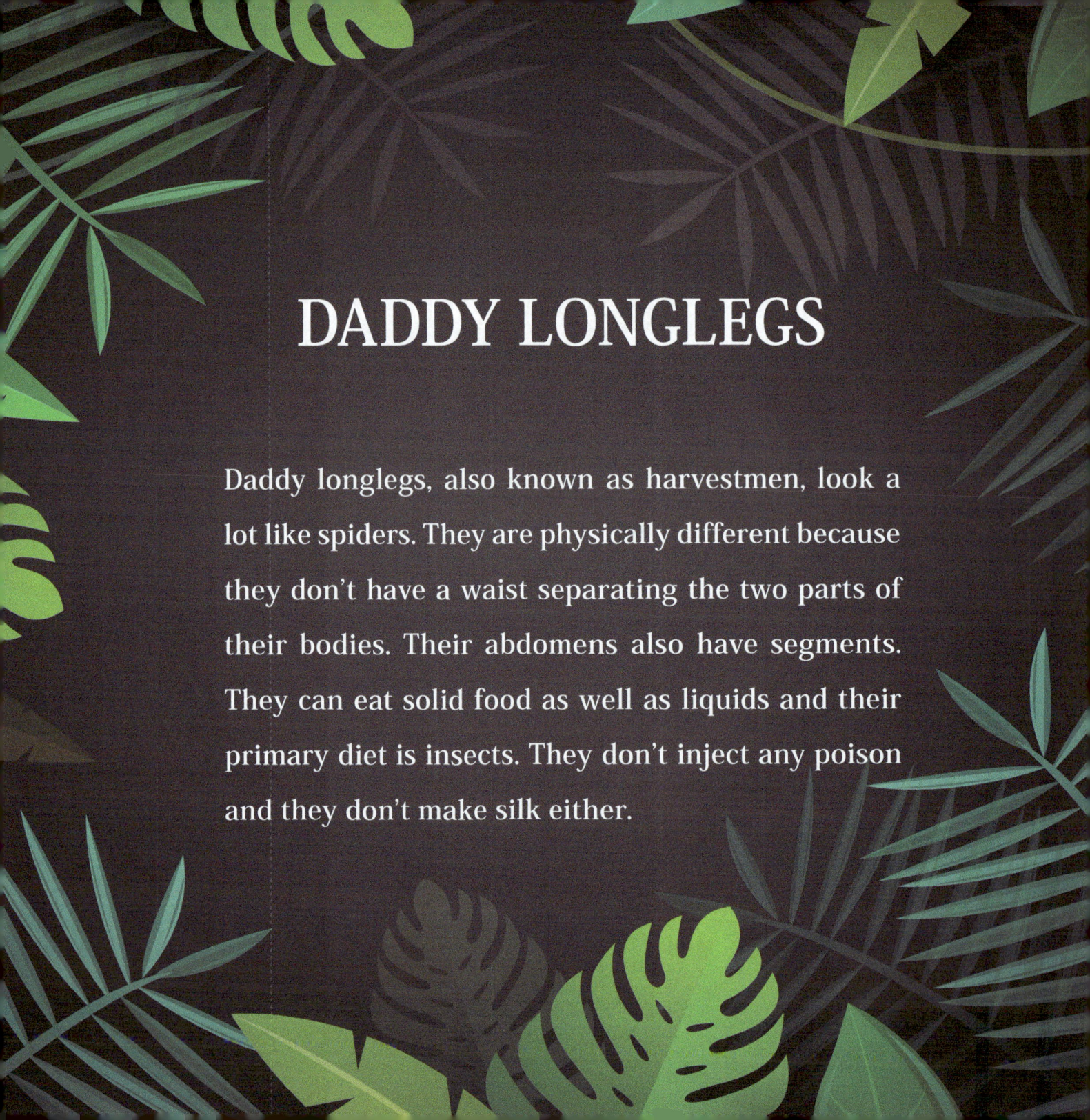

DADDY LONGLEGS

Daddy longlegs, also known as harvestmen, look a lot like spiders. They are physically different because they don't have a waist separating the two parts of their bodies. Their abdomens also have segments. They can eat solid food as well as liquids and their primary diet is insects. They don't inject any poison and they don't make silk either.

One of the techniques that daddy longlegs use is to huddle together in what looks like a giant hairy clump of hundreds of them. They can even move together as if they were one animal. Scientists don't know exactly why they do this. They might be retaining moisture in their bodies or they might be huddling together to ward off attackers.

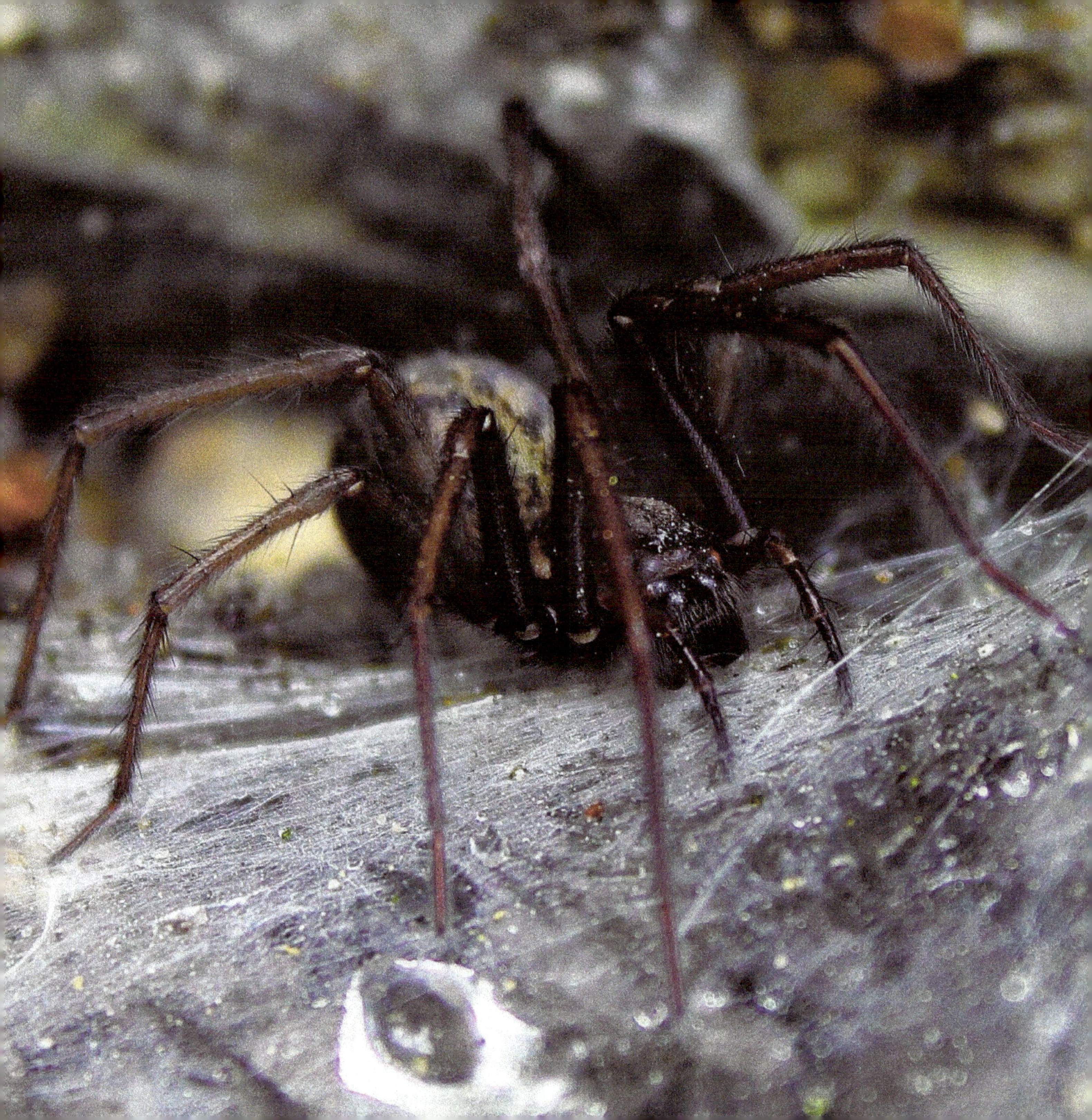

SUMMARY

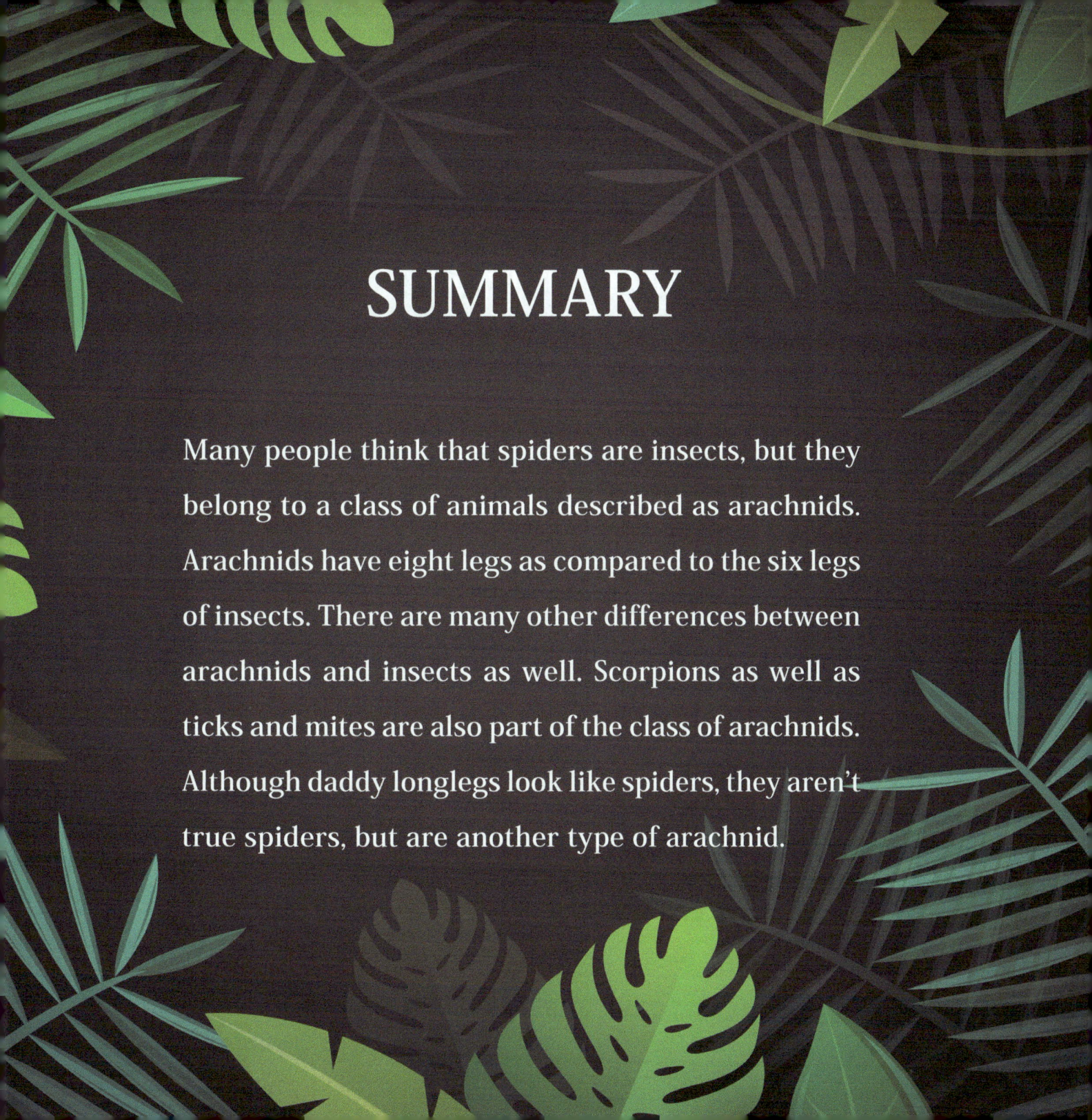

Many people think that spiders are insects, but they belong to a class of animals described as arachnids. Arachnids have eight legs as compared to the six legs of insects. There are many other differences between arachnids and insects as well. Scorpions as well as ticks and mites are also part of the class of arachnids. Although daddy longlegs look like spiders, they aren't true spiders, but are another type of arachnid.

Awesome! Now that you've read about arachnids you may want to read about amphibians and reptiles in the Baby Professor book Frogs, Snakes, Crocodiles and More | Amphibians And Reptiles for Kids | Children's Reptile & Amphibian Books.

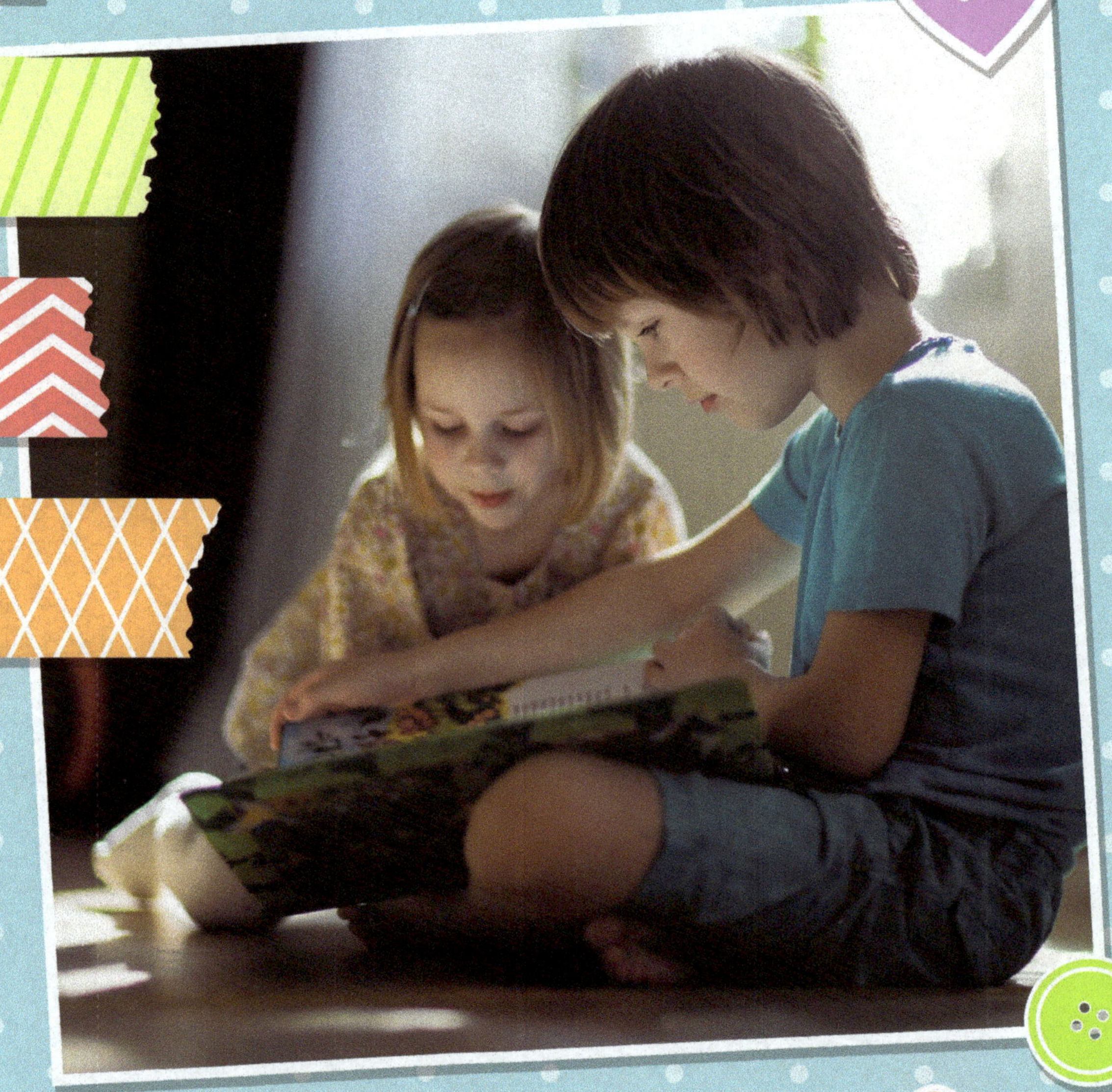

Visit

BABY PROFESSOR
EDUCATION KIDS

www.BabyProfessorBooks.com

to download Free Baby Professor eBooks
and view our catalog of new and exciting
Children's Books

Milton Keynes UK
Ingram Content Group UK Ltd.
UKHW051118030924
447530UK00025BA/11

9 798869 414113